Unstoppable You

Unstoppable You

Matthew Petchinsky

Unstoppable You: Mastering Confidence in Minutes
By: Matthew Petchinsky

Introduction: The Power of Confidence

Confidence is a transformative force. It shapes the way we see ourselves, the way we navigate the world, and how others perceive us. It's more than just standing tall or speaking boldly—it's an unshakable belief in your ability to handle whatever life throws your way. Confidence opens doors, creates opportunities, and allows you to step into your full potential. When you exude confidence, you attract success, inspire trust, and radiate a sense of control over your destiny. It's no wonder that confidence is widely regarded as the cornerstone of personal success.

But here's the truth: many of us struggle with confidence. We've all had moments of self-doubt or times when fear held us back. Whether it's speaking up in a meeting, pursuing a dream, or simply introducing yourself to someone new, a lack of confidence can keep you from living the life you deserve. The good news is that confidence isn't a fixed trait—it's a skill, one you can develop and strengthen with the right strategies.

Why Confidence is the Cornerstone of Personal Success

Confidence serves as the foundation for achievement in every aspect of life—be it your career, relationships, or personal growth. When you're confident, you're more likely to take risks, embrace challenges, and recover from setbacks. It empowers you to step out of your comfort zone, transforming fear into action and potential into results. Confidence doesn't mean you won't face difficulties; it means you'll trust yourself to handle them.

Consider how confidence impacts daily life:

- **In Your Career:** Confident individuals are more likely to advocate for themselves, ask for promotions, and take on leadership roles. They're seen as capable and trustworthy, making them magnets for opportunities.
- **In Your Relationships:** Confidence allows you to set healthy boundaries, communicate effectively, and nurture meaningful connections without fear of rejection or judgment.
- **In Personal Growth:** Confidence fuels the belief that you are capable of learning, evolving, and achieving your goals. It gives you the courage to pursue your dreams and bounce back when things don't go as planned.

The ripple effects of confidence are endless. By building your self-belief, you create a solid foundation upon which all other successes can flourish.

The Purpose of This Book: Practical Tools to Boost Confidence Instantly

The primary goal of *Unstoppable You* is to empower you with quick, practical tools to boost your confidence in minutes. This isn't a book filled with abstract theories or lengthy self-help jargon—it's a hands-on guide designed for immediate results. Whether you're preparing for a job interview, walking into a room full of strangers, or simply needing a momentary confidence boost during a challenging day, this book has you covered.

Each chapter is carefully structured to provide actionable techniques that fit seamlessly into your daily life. You'll learn how to:

- Silence your inner critic and cultivate empowering self-talk.
- Use your body language and voice to project self-assurance.
- Communicate with clarity and confidence in any situation.
- Build and maintain a reservoir of confidence that you can draw from whenever you need it.

These tools are rooted in science and tested in real-life scenarios, making them both effective and practical. The beauty of confidence is that small changes can lead to significant transformations, and this book will show you exactly how to make those changes.

Dispelling the Myths: Yes, You Can Master Confidence in Minutes

A common misconception about confidence is that it takes years to build—or worse, that you either have it or you don't. This couldn't be further from the truth. Confidence is not an innate gift bestowed upon a lucky few; it's a skill that can be learned, practiced, and mastered.

Another myth is that confidence requires perfection. Many believe that to feel confident, you must have all the answers, look a certain way, or achieve a certain level of success. In reality, confidence isn't about being perfect—it's about trusting yourself despite imperfections. It's about taking action even when you're unsure and embracing the journey rather than fearing failure.

This book is built on the premise that confidence can be created *instantly*. By understanding the psychology of confidence and learning how to access quick shifts in mindset, body language, and focus, you'll discover that building confidence is not only possible—it's surprisingly simple. With the right techniques, you can go from feeling unsure to unstoppable in just a few moments.

Confidence is your superpower, and *Unstoppable You* is your guide to unlocking it. By the end of this book, you'll not only have the tools to master confidence in minutes, but you'll also understand how to make confidence a natural, lasting part of your life. Whether you're starting your journey or looking to level up, this book will show you that unstoppable confidence is within your reach. Let's get started.

Chapter 1: The Confidence Blueprint

Confidence is often misunderstood. People mistake it for arrogance, think it requires perfection, or assume it's an elusive quality reserved for the naturally outgoing. The truth is that confidence is none of these things. It's an inner belief in your own ability to handle life's challenges, make decisions, and achieve your goals. It's not about knowing you'll succeed every time—it's about knowing you'll be okay, no matter the outcome.

In this chapter, we'll break down the essence of confidence, how it manifests in daily life, and how you can create it with intentional actions. By understanding its key components—mindset, body language, and communication—you'll uncover the secrets to building a powerful and lasting sense of self-assurance. Finally, we'll explore the science behind quick confidence shifts, giving you practical tools to change your state instantly.

Understanding What Confidence Truly Is

Confidence isn't a single trait or quality—it's a dynamic state of being that influences how you think, feel, and act. It's the foundation of resilience, allowing you to face challenges head-on and adapt when things don't go as planned. At its core, confidence is about trust: trust in yourself, your abilities, and your capacity to learn and grow.

How Confidence Manifests in Daily Life:

- **Decision-Making:** Confident individuals trust their judgment, even when faced with uncertainty. They make choices decisively and accept the outcomes as opportunities to learn and grow.
- **Risk-Taking:** Confidence encourages you to step outside your comfort zone, take calculated risks, and embrace opportunities. It helps you overcome the fear of failure or rejection.
- **Resilience:** Confidence acts as a buffer against setbacks. When things go wrong, confident people are more likely to bounce back quickly and maintain a positive outlook.
- **Interpersonal Interactions:** Confidence makes you approachable, assertive, and engaging. It helps you express your thoughts clearly, set boundaries, and build meaningful relationships.
- **Self-Care and Growth:** When you believe in yourself, you're more likely to prioritize your well-being and invest in personal development.

Confidence isn't static. It can ebb and flow depending on the situation, your mood, and external circumstances. The good news is that confidence is a skill, and like any skill, it can be cultivated and strengthened with practice.

Breaking Down the Components of Confidence

To build unshakable confidence, it's essential to understand its three core components: mindset, body language, and communication. Each of these elements plays a crucial role in how confidence is perceived—both by yourself and by others.

1. Mindset: The Foundation of Confidence Your mindset is the internal dialogue and beliefs that shape your perception of yourself and the world. A confident mindset is rooted in self-acceptance and growth, not perfection. It's about reframing challenges as opportunities and believing in your ability to adapt and succeed.

- **Fixed vs. Growth Mindset:** A fixed mindset believes that abilities are static, while a growth mindset embraces the idea that skills and talents can be developed. Confidence thrives in a growth mindset.
- **Self-Talk:** Your inner dialogue is a powerful force. Positive self-talk, such as affirmations or encouraging statements, can significantly boost your confidence.
- **Visualization:** Mentally rehearsing success can program your mind to believe in positive outcomes. Visualization is a proven technique for boosting confidence before high-pressure situations.

2. Body Language: Speaking Without Words Your body language communicates confidence (or lack thereof) long before you say a word. The way you stand, move, and gesture sends powerful signals to both your brain and those around you.

- **Posture:** Standing tall with your shoulders back signals self-assurance. Slouching, on the other hand, conveys uncertainty.
- **Gestures:** Open, expansive gestures exude confidence, while closed or hesitant movements suggest insecurity.
- **Eye Contact:** Maintaining steady eye contact shows that you're engaged and confident. Avoiding eye contact can give the impression of nervousness or doubt.
- **Power Poses:** Research by social psychologist Amy Cuddy shows that adopting power poses for just two minutes can elevate confidence and reduce stress.

3. Communication: Confidence in Action The words you use and how you deliver them are critical aspects of confidence. Confident communication isn't about dominating a conversation—it's about clarity, authenticity, and connection.

- **Tone of Voice:** A calm, steady tone conveys control and self-assurance. Speaking too quickly or softly can undermine confidence.
- **Pacing:** Speaking at a deliberate pace shows thoughtfulness and composure. Rushing through sentences can signal nervousness.
- **Clarity:** Confident communicators are clear and concise. They avoid filler words like "um" or "like" and focus on delivering their message effectively.

The Science Behind Quick Confidence Shifts

Confidence may seem intangible, but it has a biological basis. By understanding how your brain works, you can use science-backed techniques to create rapid shifts in your confidence levels.

1. Harnessing Neuroplasticity

Neuroplasticity is the brain's ability to reorganize itself by forming new neural connections. This means you can train your brain to adopt more confident thought patterns. Each time you practice confidence-building techniques, you strengthen these neural pathways, making confidence a natural response.

2. Instant Confidence Triggers

Certain actions and mental shifts can create an immediate sense of confidence. These include:

- **Anchoring:** This NLP (Neuro-Linguistic Programming) technique involves associating a confident state with a physical gesture (e.g., squeezing your fist) so you can trigger confidence on demand.
- **Power Breathing:** Slow, deep breaths signal your brain to relax, reducing anxiety and creating a sense of control.
- **Gratitude Practice:** Shifting your focus to what you're grateful for can instantly elevate your mood and confidence by shifting your perspective to abundance rather than lack.

3. The Role of Hormones

Confidence is influenced by the hormones cortisol (stress hormone) and testosterone (dominance hormone). Simple techniques like power poses, deep breathing, and positive visualization can lower cortisol and increase testosterone, creating a physiological boost in confidence.

4. The Feedback Loop of Confidence

Confidence is self-reinforcing. When you act confidently, you receive positive feedback from the world around you, which reinforces your belief in yourself. Over time, this creates a virtuous cycle where confidence becomes your default state.

Confidence is not reserved for a select few—it's a skill anyone can master. By understanding what confidence truly is and breaking it down into its key components, you can begin to rebuild your foundation of self-assurance. Armed with the science of quick confidence shifts, you'll discover that becoming unstoppable is not only possible—it's inevitable.

Chapter 2: Mastering Your Inner Dialogue

Your inner dialogue is the most influential voice in your life. It narrates your experiences, shapes your beliefs, and influences how you respond to challenges. For many of us, this voice can be overly critical, dwelling on mistakes and magnifying fears. The inner critic, while often a product of past experiences and self-doubt, can become a significant roadblock to confidence if left unchecked. Mastering your inner dialogue means learning to identify and silence that inner critic, reframing negative thoughts, and cultivating empowering beliefs that fuel self-assurance.

This chapter will guide you through the process of transforming your inner dialogue from a harsh critic to a supportive coach, using actionable exercises, affirmations, and visualization techniques.

Identifying and Silencing Your Inner Critic in Moments

The inner critic is that nagging voice that tells you you're not good enough, smart enough, or capable enough. While it often masquerades as a form of self-protection—trying to keep you from failure or embarrassment—it usually ends up holding you back.

Recognizing the Inner Critic

The first step in silencing your inner critic is recognizing its voice. The inner critic often uses:

- **Absolute Statements:** Words like "always," "never," and "can't" (e.g., "You always mess things up," or "You can't handle this.").
- **Catastrophic Thinking:** Jumping to the worst-case scenario without evidence (e.g., "If you fail this presentation, your career is over.").
- **Personal Attacks:** Criticizing your worth or abilities (e.g., "You're so stupid," or "No one takes you seriously.").

Steps to Silence Your Inner Critic

1. **Name the Critic:** Give your inner critic a name or persona to separate it from your true self. For example, you might call it "Doubtful Debbie" or "Negative Ned." This creates emotional distance and helps you recognize it as just one perspective, not the truth.
2. **Pause and Acknowledge:** When the inner critic pipes up, pause and acknowledge its presence. Say to yourself, "That's my inner critic talking. It's not me."
3. **Challenge the Critic:** Ask yourself:
     - *Is this thought based on facts or assumptions?*
     - *What's the worst-case scenario, and how likely is it?*
     - *What would I say to a friend who had this thought?*
4. **Replace with Truth:** Replace the critical thought with a more balanced, constructive one. For example:
     - Instead of: "You'll never get this right," say: "I might not be perfect, but I'm capable of learning and improving."

Simple Exercises to Reframe Negative Thoughts into Empowering Ones

Reframing is the process of shifting your perspective on a thought or situation to see it in a more positive or constructive light. It doesn't mean ignoring challenges but choosing a perspective that empowers rather than limits you.

The Reframing Process

1. **Identify the Negative Thought:** Write it down. Seeing the thought on paper helps you assess it more objectively.
2. **Examine the Evidence:** Ask yourself:
    - What evidence supports this thought?
    - What evidence contradicts it?
3. **Ask an Empowering Question:** Shift your focus by asking:
    - *What's another way to look at this situation?*
    - *What's the lesson or opportunity here?*
4. **Create a New Narrative:** Rewrite the thought in a way that encourages growth and confidence.

Example Exercise: The Thought Flip

1. Write down a negative thought, such as, "I'm terrible at public speaking."
2. Flip it into a positive statement that acknowledges effort or potential, such as, "I'm improving my public speaking skills every time I practice."
3. Repeat the flipped thought aloud until it feels more believable.

Mindset Journal

- Each evening, write down three negative thoughts you noticed during the day.
- For each thought, reframe it into a positive or constructive perspective.
- Over time, this practice rewires your brain to naturally focus on empowering thoughts.

Affirmations and Visualization Techniques to Shift Self-Perception

Affirmations and visualization are powerful tools for rewiring your inner dialogue and boosting your self-confidence. They work by creating mental patterns that align with the confident, capable version of yourself you want to embody.

Affirmations: Rewriting Your Mental Script

Affirmations are positive statements designed to challenge and replace negative beliefs. To be effective, they should be:

- **Personal:** Use "I" statements (e.g., "I am confident," "I am capable of achieving my goals.").
- **Present-Tense:** Phrase them as if the desired outcome is already true (e.g., "I am calm and prepared for this presentation.").
- **Believable:** Start with affirmations that feel realistic and gradually build toward more aspirational ones.

Examples of Confidence-Boosting Affirmations:

- "I trust myself to handle whatever comes my way."
- "I am worthy of success and happiness."
- "I am constantly growing and improving."
- "I am confident, capable, and ready to shine."

How to Use Affirmations:

- Repeat them aloud or silently during moments of self-doubt.
- Write them on sticky notes and place them where you'll see them frequently (e.g., on your mirror or desk).
- Combine affirmations with deep breathing to anchor them more deeply in your mind.

Visualization: Creating a Mental Blueprint of Confidence

Visualization involves imagining yourself successfully navigating a situation or embodying the qualities you desire. It primes your brain for success and helps you feel more prepared.

Steps for Effective Visualization:

1. **Find a Quiet Space:** Sit in a comfortable position and close your eyes.
2. **Create a Detailed Scene:** Imagine a specific scenario where you want to feel confident (e.g., giving a presentation, meeting someone new).
    - Visualize the setting, the people around you, and your actions.
    - Picture yourself standing tall, speaking clearly, and feeling calm and composed.
3. **Engage Your Senses:** Focus on what you see, hear, and feel in this moment of confidence. The more vivid the visualization, the more effective it will be.
4. **Embrace the Emotion:** As you visualize, allow yourself to feel the emotions of confidence, pride, and success.

Daily Practice: The Confidence Visualization

- Spend 5 minutes each morning visualizing yourself confidently handling your biggest challenge of the day. This primes your brain to approach the situation with self-assurance.

Mastering your inner dialogue is about taking control of the voice in your head and aligning it with the version of yourself you want to become. By identifying and silencing your inner critic, reframing negative thoughts, and practicing affirmations and visualization, you can shift your self-perception and unlock the confidence that's already within you. Confidence isn't just about what you do—it's about how you think and feel about yourself. By mastering your inner dialogue, you'll lay the foundation for unstoppable self-belief.

Chapter 3: Body Language Boosters

Body language is a silent yet powerful tool for building and projecting confidence. It communicates your emotional state, level of self-assurance, and how others perceive you—all without a single word. Studies suggest that as much as 70-93% of communication is nonverbal, making your posture, movements, and expressions critical to how you're perceived by others and how you feel about yourself.

In this chapter, we'll explore how small adjustments in posture and movement can instantly boost your confidence. You'll learn about power poses, breathing techniques, and micro-adjustments that exude self-assurance. Finally, we'll provide quick, actionable tips to command presence in any situation, whether it's a high-stakes interview, a crucial meeting, or a social gathering.

The Immediate Impact of Posture and Physical Movement on Confidence

Your body language doesn't just reflect your inner state—it also shapes it. This phenomenon, known as the "body-mind connection," means that how you carry yourself can influence how you feel. Slouching, crossing your arms, or avoiding eye contact can make you feel insecure, while standing tall and open can create a sense of self-assurance.

The Science Behind Body Language and Confidence

- **Amy Cuddy's Research on Power Posing:** Social psychologist Amy Cuddy demonstrated that adopting expansive, open postures (like standing with your arms wide) can increase testosterone (associated with dominance) and decrease cortisol (associated with stress). These hormonal changes can make you feel more confident within just two minutes.
- **Feedback Loop of Body Language:** When you adopt confident body language, others perceive you as confident and respond accordingly, reinforcing your self-assurance.

Common Postural Habits That Undermine Confidence

- **Slouching:** Collapsed posture signals insecurity and low energy.
- **Fidgeting:** Excessive movement conveys nervousness and distracts from your message.
- **Avoiding Eye Contact:** Looking away can make you appear uncertain or disengaged.

Confident Posture: A Quick Checklist

- **Stand Tall:** Keep your shoulders back, chest slightly lifted, and spine straight.
- **Feet Placement:** Stand with your feet shoulder-width apart to create a stable and grounded appearance.
- **Relax Your Hands:** Avoid clenching your fists or crossing your arms; let your hands rest naturally at your sides or use open gestures.
- **Face Forward:** Maintain a neutral head position, with your chin parallel to the ground.

Power Poses, Breathing Techniques, and Micro-Adjustments to Exude Self-Assurance
Power Poses: Building Confidence in Two Minutes
Power poses are expansive stances that create a sense of control and authority. Practicing these poses before a challenging situation can significantly boost your confidence.

Examples of Power Poses:

1. **The Wonder Woman Pose:** Stand tall with your hands on your hips, feet shoulder-width apart, and chest slightly lifted.
2. **The Victory Pose:** Raise your arms in a V-shape above your head, as if celebrating a win.
3. **The CEO Pose:** Sit back in a chair with your arms resting behind your head and feet planted firmly on the floor.

How to Use Power Poses:

- Find a private space to practice these poses for two minutes before a meeting, presentation, or social event.
- Focus on your breathing while holding the pose to enhance its calming and empowering effects.

Breathing Techniques: Controlling Nerves and Exuding Calm
Your breath is a powerful regulator of your emotional state. When you're nervous, your breathing becomes shallow and quick, signaling stress to your brain. By slowing and deepening your breath, you can calm your nerves and project confidence.

Techniques for Confident Breathing:

1. **Diaphragmatic Breathing (Belly Breathing):** Inhale deeply through your nose, letting your belly expand, then exhale slowly through your mouth. This activates the parasympathetic nervous system, reducing stress.
2. **Box Breathing:** Inhale for four counts, hold for four counts, exhale for four counts, and hold for four counts. Repeat this cycle to regain composure and focus.
3. **Sigh Technique:** Take a deep breath, then release it with an audible sigh. This helps release tension and reset your energy.

Micro-Adjustments for Instant Confidence

Sometimes, small tweaks to your body language can make a big difference in how you're perceived. These micro-adjustments are quick and easy to implement.

- **Relax Your Shoulders:** Tension in your shoulders can make you appear stressed. Roll them back and down to create a relaxed, open posture.
- **Open Your Hands:** Use open-palmed gestures to convey honesty and approachability.
- **Smile Naturally:** A genuine smile not only makes you appear confident but also triggers the release of endorphins, boosting your mood.
- **Maintain Eye Contact:** Aim to hold eye contact for 3-5 seconds before looking away. This creates a sense of connection without feeling intimidating.

Quick Tips for Commanding Presence in Any Situation

Whether you're walking into an interview, leading a meeting, or mingling at a social event, your body language plays a critical role in how others perceive you. These tips will help you make a lasting impression and exude confidence effortlessly.

In Interviews

- **Walk in with Purpose:** Enter the room with steady steps, making eye contact with those present.
- **Handshake:** Offer a firm but not overpowering handshake, maintaining eye contact and smiling.

- **Sit Confidently:** Sit with your back straight and hands resting lightly on the table or in your lap. Avoid slouching or leaning back excessively.
- **Mirror Body Language:** Subtly mirror the interviewer's posture and gestures to build rapport.

In Meetings

- **Claim Your Space:** Sit at the table rather than on the sidelines, and avoid shrinking into your chair.
- **Use Gestures Thoughtfully:** Use deliberate hand movements to emphasize key points without overdoing it.
- **Pause for Effect:** When speaking, pause briefly after key statements to convey authority and allow your message to sink in.

In Social Events

- **Approach with Confidence:** Walk up to groups with a smile and introduce yourself confidently.
- **Stand Openly:** Avoid crossing your arms or turning your body away from the group.
- **Engage with Your Eyes:** Make eye contact with each person in the group as you speak, showing inclusivity.
- **Tilt Your Head Slightly:** A slight head tilt signals attentiveness and warmth.

Universal Tips for Any Setting

- **Own the Room:** Visualize yourself as someone who belongs and has something valuable to offer.
- **Pace Yourself:** Speak slowly and deliberately to convey calm and control.

- **Avoid Fidgeting:** Keep your hands steady and movements purposeful to project composure.

Mastering your body language is one of the fastest and most effective ways to build confidence. By understanding the immediate impact of posture and movement, practicing power poses, and applying simple breathing techniques, you can transform how you feel and how others perceive you. With these tools in your arsenal, you'll be ready to command presence and exude self-assurance in any situation. Confidence isn't just in your mind—it's in the way you move.

Chapter 4: Communicate Like a Pro

Confidence isn't just about how you feel—it's also about how you express yourself. The way you speak directly affects how confident you appear and, in turn, how confident you feel. Effective communication is a key skill that can open doors in your personal and professional life. Whether you're presenting in a meeting, networking at an event, or simply making small talk, how you communicate shapes others' perceptions of you and reinforces your own self-assurance.

In this chapter, we'll explore the connection between speaking and confidence, provide strategies for speaking clearly and assertively, and share quick conversation hacks to help you overcome social anxiety.

The Link Between How You Speak and How Confident You Feel

Your voice is one of the most powerful tools for projecting confidence. When you speak with clarity and conviction, you're more likely to be perceived as confident and capable. Conversely, hesitations, fillers (like "um" or "uh"), and a shaky tone can undermine your message, even if your content is strong.

How Speaking Affects Your Confidence

1. **Feedback Loop:** The way you speak influences how others respond to you. Positive reactions from your audience reinforce your confidence, creating a virtuous cycle.
2. **Physiological Impact:** Speaking clearly and at a controlled pace helps regulate your breathing and reduce anxiety, making you feel more in control.
3. **Psychological Alignment:** Speaking with confidence aligns your external expression with your internal state, creating a sense of authenticity and self-assurance.

Common Barriers to Confident Speech

- Fear of judgment or rejection.
- Overthinking your words, leading to hesitations or stumbling.
- Speaking too quickly due to nerves.
- A tendency to downplay your opinions or soften your statements to avoid conflict.

Understanding these barriers is the first step toward overcoming them. The good news is that with practice and the right strategies, you can train yourself to speak like a pro, even in high-pressure situations.

Strategies for Speaking Clearly, Confidently, and Assertively

1. Clarity: Make Your Message Heard

Clarity ensures that your audience understands your message. Confident speakers prioritize simplicity and structure over overly complex language or rambling explanations.

- **Organize Your Thoughts:** Before speaking, take a moment to mentally outline what you want to say. Use a structure like:
  - **Point:** State your main idea clearly.
  - **Example:** Provide a supporting example or explanation.
  - **Conclusion:** Summarize or emphasize your main point.
- **Eliminate Filler Words:** Practice replacing "um," "uh," "like," and "you know" with pauses. A brief silence is more impactful than a filler word.
- **Be Concise:** Avoid over-explaining or repeating yourself unnecessarily. Aim to deliver your message in as few words as possible while maintaining depth.

2. Confidence: Own Your Voice

Confidence in speech comes from how you deliver your words, not just what you say.

- **Control Your Tone:** Speak with a steady, calm tone that conveys authority. Avoid speaking too softly, which can make you seem uncertain, or too loudly, which can come across as aggressive.
- **Pace Yourself:** Speaking too quickly signals nervousness. Practice speaking at a deliberate pace, with natural pauses for emphasis.
- **Project Your Voice:** Ensure your voice carries to the entire room or group without shouting. Proper breathing techniques, like diaphragmatic breathing, help you project effectively.

- **Emphasize Key Points:** Use vocal variety (changing pitch, volume, or speed) to highlight important ideas and keep your audience engaged.

3. Assertiveness: Speak with Authority

Assertive communication strikes a balance between passivity and aggression. It shows that you respect both yourself and others.

- **Use "I" Statements:** Frame your thoughts and feelings in terms of your own perspective (e.g., "I believe," "I feel," "I suggest"). This reduces defensiveness while showing self-assurance.
- **Avoid Qualifiers:** Phrases like "I think," "I guess," or "maybe" weaken your message. Replace them with direct statements, such as "I recommend" or "I believe this approach works."
- **Stand by Your Opinions:** Confidence doesn't require you to be infallible. If challenged, calmly explain your reasoning or acknowledge opposing views without backing down unnecessarily.

Overcoming Social Anxiety with Quick Conversation Hacks

Social anxiety can make speaking in groups, starting conversations, or presenting your ideas feel overwhelming. However, with the right techniques, you can navigate these situations with ease.

1. Start with Simple Icebreakers

If initiating conversation feels daunting, prepare a few go-to ice-breakers. These should be open-ended questions that invite the other person to share their thoughts. Examples include:

- "What brings you to this event?"
- "How did you get into your field?"
- "What's the most interesting thing you've worked on recently?"

Starting with curiosity shifts the focus away from yourself and reduces pressure.

2. Use Active Listening

Active listening not only keeps the conversation flowing but also builds rapport and shows confidence.

- **Paraphrase and Reflect:** Repeat or paraphrase what the other person said to show engagement (e.g., "So you've been working on that project for six months—that sounds intense!").
- **Ask Follow-Up Questions:** This deepens the conversation and reduces the need to come up with entirely new topics.

3. Practice the "Spotlight Effect" Mindset Shift

Social anxiety often stems from the belief that everyone is scrutinizing you. In reality, most people are focused on themselves.

- **Reframe Your Focus:** Instead of worrying about how you're being perceived, focus on making the other person feel comfortable or engaged.
- **Adopt a Helper's Mindset:** Think of yourself as contributing value to the interaction rather than being judged.

4. The Three-Second Rule

When you feel nervous about starting a conversation, count to three and take action. This short-circuits overthinking and gets you into the flow of interaction before anxiety builds.

5. Prepare for Common Scenarios

Anticipate situations that trigger anxiety and rehearse your responses. For example:

- If someone asks, "What do you do?" have a concise and confident answer ready.
- Practice introducing yourself with a brief, engaging pitch.

Practical Exercises to Build Communication Confidence

1. **Mirror Practice:** Stand in front of a mirror and practice delivering a short message. Pay attention to your tone, posture, and facial expressions. Adjust as needed until you project confidence.
2. **Record and Review:** Record yourself speaking on a topic, then play it back to identify areas for improvement in tone, pacing, and clarity.
3. **Improv Practice:** Engage in improvisational speaking exercises, such as joining a Toastmasters club or practicing with friends. The ability to think on your feet builds confidence.

4. **Progressive Exposure:** Gradually increase your exposure to challenging communication situations. Start with low-pressure settings, like small group conversations, before tackling larger audiences.

Speaking confidently is a skill that anyone can master. By understanding the link between how you speak and how confident you feel, implementing strategies for clarity and assertiveness, and using simple hacks to overcome social anxiety, you'll unlock the ability to communicate like a pro in any situation. Confidence isn't just about what you say—it's about how you say it, and now, you're equipped to let your voice shine.

Chapter 5: Building Confidence Momentum

Confidence, like a muscle, grows stronger with consistent use and reinforcement. While it's possible to create confidence instantly in moments of need, maintaining and growing it requires regular practice. The goal is to transform confidence from something you summon occasionally into a natural and habitual state of being.

In this chapter, we'll explore how to sustain and grow your confidence with minimal daily effort, create a personalized "confidence toolkit" for any situation, and develop habits that make confidence feel effortless and second nature.

How to Maintain and Grow Confidence with Minimal Daily Effort

Sustaining confidence doesn't have to involve dramatic changes to your routine. Small, consistent actions can yield significant results over time, creating a foundation of self-assurance that strengthens naturally.

1. The Power of Small Wins

Confidence is built through achievements, no matter how small. Setting and accomplishing minor daily goals reinforces your belief in your abilities.

- **Start Your Day with Intention:** Identify one small, achievable goal each morning (e.g., making a call you've been putting off or organizing your workspace). Completing it sets a positive tone for the day and builds momentum.
- **Celebrate Progress:** Acknowledge and celebrate your successes, no matter how minor. This reinforces a positive feedback loop and motivates you to tackle bigger challenges.

2. Daily Affirmation Ritual

Repetition is key to rewiring your brain for confidence. By repeating affirmations daily, you reinforce empowering beliefs.

- **Morning Affirmations:** Start each day by repeating three to five affirmations aloud. Example: "I am capable of handling anything that comes my way."
- **Gratitude and Reflection:** At the end of the day, reflect on moments when you felt confident or achieved something. Gratitude reinforces a positive mindset.

3. Body Language Practices

Your posture and physical presence influence your mental state throughout the day.

- **Posture Check-Ins:** Set reminders to check your posture periodically. Adjust to a tall, open stance to maintain confidence in how you feel and appear.
- **Power Poses:** Incorporate a 2-minute power pose into your morning or pre-event routine.

4. Regular Self-Reflection

Self-awareness is critical to maintaining and growing confidence.

- **Confidence Journal:** Spend 5-10 minutes journaling about situations where you felt confident and analyzing why. Identify patterns and areas for growth.
- **Learn from Setbacks:** When confidence falters, use it as a learning opportunity. Ask yourself, "What can I take away from this experience?"

5. Consistent Skill Development

Confidence grows when you challenge yourself to improve in meaningful ways.

- **Master Your Craft:** Dedicate time to honing skills in areas that matter to you, whether professionally or personally. Competence breeds confidence.
- **Try New Experiences:** Regularly step outside your comfort zone to build resilience and adaptability.

Developing a "Confidence Toolkit" for Every Occasion

A confidence toolkit is a personalized set of strategies, techniques, and resources you can draw on in any situation. This toolkit ensures you're always prepared to handle challenges with poise and self-assurance.

Essential Components of Your Toolkit

1. **Affirmations and Mantras:** Have a list of go-to affirmations that resonate with you. Examples:
   - "I've got this."
   - "I am enough."
   - "Challenges are opportunities to grow."
2. **Visualization Exercises:** Practice visualizing successful outcomes for situations you frequently encounter, such as presentations, interviews, or social interactions.
3. **Power Poses and Breathing Techniques:** Develop a shortlist of poses and breathing exercises that help you calm nerves and feel grounded.
4. **Confidence Anchors:** Use objects or gestures to remind yourself of past successes. For example:
   - A piece of jewelry or accessory associated with a significant achievement.
   - A gesture like squeezing your fist to anchor feelings of power and control.
5. **Conversation Starters:** Prepare a set of versatile questions or topics to break the ice in social situations.
6. **Go-To Outfits:** Wear clothing that makes you feel confident and polished. A well-fitting outfit can boost your mood and presence instantly.
7. **Support Network:** Surround yourself with people who encourage and uplift you. Knowing you have a support system boosts your confidence during challenging times.

Customizing Your Toolkit for Different Scenarios

- **Professional Settings:** Focus on clarity of thought, assertive body language, and prepared responses.
- **Social Events:** Emphasize active listening, approachable posture, and icebreakers.
- **Personal Challenges:** Rely on affirmations, reflective journaling, and support from trusted friends or mentors.

Turning Confidence into a Habit That Feels Effortless and Natural

True confidence isn't something you consciously think about—it's an ingrained part of your character. By forming habits that prioritize self-assurance, you can make confidence second nature.

1. Build a Confidence Routine

Incorporate daily and weekly habits that reinforce your confidence.

- **Morning Confidence Ritual:** Start each day with an affirmation, power pose, or visualization exercise.
- **Weekly Reflection:** Set aside time to review your achievements and identify areas for growth.

2. Replace Negative Habits with Positive Ones

Identify habits that undermine your confidence, such as negative self-talk or procrastination, and replace them with empowering practices.

- **Shift Self-Talk:** Every time you catch yourself thinking, "I can't," reframe it as, "I'm learning how to."
- **Proactive Action:** Break tasks into smaller steps to overcome procrastination and create a sense of accomplishment.

3. Surround Yourself with Positivity

Your environment and relationships play a significant role in shaping your confidence.

- **Curate Your Environment:** Fill your space with items, quotes, or images that inspire you.
- **Choose Supportive Relationships:** Spend time with people who believe in your potential and encourage you to take risks.

4. Use the "2% Rule"

Make small, consistent improvements in your confidence every day. For example:

- Speak up 2% more in meetings.
- Hold eye contact 2% longer in conversations.
- Push yourself 2% further outside your comfort zone in new situations.

5. Practice Confidence Until It's Automatic

Repetition is the key to making confidence a habit. The more you practice speaking up, taking initiative, and maintaining empowering body language, the more natural it becomes.

Practical Exercises for Building Confidence Momentum

1. **The "Three Wins" Exercise:** At the end of each day, write down three things you did well. This reinforces a positive self-image and builds momentum for the next day.
2. **Confidence Stacking:** Begin your day with a small, confidence-boosting activity (e.g., completing a task or dressing sharply) and build on that energy throughout the day.
3. **Weekly Challenge:** Set a weekly goal to do one thing outside your comfort zone. Reflect on how it felt and what you learned.

Sustaining Confidence Long-Term

Confidence is a journey, not a destination. By maintaining consistent habits, preparing with your confidence toolkit, and celebrating your growth, you can create a lasting foundation of self-assurance. Over time, confidence will become an integral part of your identity—something you naturally exude in every area of your life.

With the strategies in this chapter, you're no longer relying on fleeting moments of confidence. Instead, you're cultivating a state of being that empowers you to face any challenge with resilience, poise, and unshakable belief in yourself.

Appendix A: Your Quick Confidence Cheat Sheet

This appendix is your go-to resource for instantly boosting your confidence, expanding your knowledge, and overcoming common challenges. Designed as a practical reference, it provides quick steps to regain self-assurance in just minutes, a curated list of tools and books to deepen your mastery, and answers to frequently asked questions about confidence-building.

Step-by-Step Guide to Boosting Confidence in Under 5 Minutes

Confidence can be summoned quickly with the right combination of mental, physical, and emotional shifts. Follow these steps anytime you need an instant boost:

Step 1: Take Control of Your Posture (1 Minute)

- Stand tall, feet shoulder-width apart, shoulders back, and chest slightly lifted.
- Assume a power pose such as the **Wonder Woman Pose** (hands on hips) or **Victory Pose** (arms raised in a V-shape above your head).
- Hold this position for 1 minute while breathing deeply.

Step 2: Focus on Your Breath (1-2 Minutes)

- Practice **diaphragmatic breathing**:
  1. Inhale deeply through your nose for 4 counts, letting your belly expand.
  2. Hold your breath for 4 counts.
  3. Exhale slowly through your mouth for 6-8 counts.
  4. Repeat 3-5 cycles to calm your nerves and center your mind.

Step 3: Reframe Your Inner Dialogue (1 Minute)

- Identify any negative thoughts causing doubt (e.g., "I'm not ready for this").
- Replace them with empowering affirmations such as:
    - "I am capable and prepared."
    - "I've overcome challenges like this before, and I can do it again."
    - "I belong here, and I've got this."

Step 4: Visualize Success (1 Minute)

- Close your eyes and picture yourself succeeding in the situation ahead.
- Imagine the setting, your actions, and the positive outcome in vivid detail.
- Feel the emotions of confidence and pride as if you've already succeeded.

Step 5: Make a Small Physical Adjustment (30 Seconds)

- Smile naturally—this triggers positive emotions in your brain.
- Roll your shoulders back and down to release tension.
- Adjust your outfit or posture to feel polished and put-together.

By combining these steps, you'll feel calmer, more focused, and ready to tackle any challenge in just 5 minutes.

Recommended Books, Tools, and Additional Resources
To deepen your understanding of confidence and continue your growth, here's a curated list of highly recommended resources:
Books on Confidence and Personal Development

1. **"The Confidence Code" by Katty Kay and Claire Shipman**
   ○ Explores the science and art of confidence, with actionable insights for developing self-assurance.
2. **"Presence: Bringing Your Boldest Self to Your Biggest Challenges" by Amy Cuddy**
   ○ Details the power of body language and techniques like power posing to boost confidence.
3. **"Feel the Fear and Do It Anyway" by Susan Jeffers**
   ○ Teaches strategies for overcoming fear and embracing challenges with courage.
4. **"Daring Greatly" by Brené Brown**
   ○ Focuses on the link between vulnerability and true confidence.
5. **"You Are a Badass" by Jen Sincero**
   ○ A motivational guide to embracing your strengths and living a confident life.

Online Tools and Resources

- **TED Talks:**
  - *Amy Cuddy's "Your Body Language Shapes Who You Are"*
  - *Mel Robbins' "How to Stop Screwing Yourself Over"*
- **Confidence Apps:**
  - *Headspace* (for mindfulness and calming nerves)
  - *ThinkUp* (for personalized affirmations)
- **Online Courses:**
  - *"Confidence Coaching" on Udemy or Skillshare*
  - *"Art of Communicating with Confidence" on LinkedIn Learning*

Confidence-Building Communities

- **Toastmasters International:** A supportive environment to practice public speaking and leadership skills.
- **Meetup Groups:** Join confidence-focused meetups or personal growth workshops in your area.

FAQs: Common Confidence Challenges and Quick Solutions
1. What if I feel nervous before a big event?

- **Solution:** Use the 5-minute confidence routine outlined above. Pay special attention to diaphragmatic breathing and visualization. Remind yourself that nerves are a natural response and can fuel your energy if you channel them positively.

2. How can I stay confident when receiving criticism?

- **Solution:** Pause before responding. Thank the person for their feedback and view it as an opportunity to grow. Reframe criticism as constructive input rather than a personal attack.

3. How do I handle situations where I feel out of my depth?

- **Solution:** Focus on what you *do* know or can contribute. Use phrases like, "I'll look into that and get back to you" to show confidence without pretending to have all the answers.

4. What if I struggle with confidence in social settings?

- **Solution:** Prepare a few conversation starters in advance. Focus on active listening and showing genuine curiosity about others. Remember the *spotlight effect*—people are usually more focused on themselves than on you.

5. How can I rebuild confidence after a failure?

- **Solution:** Reflect on what you've learned from the experience and focus on your progress rather than perfection. Write down past successes to remind yourself of your capabilities.

6. How do I avoid comparing myself to others?

- **Solution:** Shift your focus inward. Celebrate your unique strengths and achievements. Remind yourself that everyone has their own journey, and comparison doesn't serve your growth.

7. How do I stay confident in high-pressure situations?

- **Solution:** Break the situation into smaller, manageable steps. Use power poses and controlled breathing to calm your nerves. Focus on the task at hand rather than the outcome.

8. Can confidence be sustained long-term without constant effort?

- **Solution:** Yes, by developing confidence habits. Regularly practice affirmations, reflect on your wins, and challenge yourself to step outside your comfort zone. Over time, these actions will make confidence an automatic part of your life.

This cheat sheet is designed to be your confidence-boosting companion. Whether you're preparing for a big presentation, navigating a social event, or facing personal challenges, these tools and resources will help you build unshakable self-assurance and become unstoppable in every aspect of your life.

Message from the Author:

I hope you enjoyed this book, I love astrology and knew there was not a book such as this out on the shelf. I love metaphysical items as well. Please check out my other books:

-Life of Government Benefits

-My life of Hell

-My life with Hydrocephalus

-Red Sky

-World Domination:Woman's rule

-World Domination:Woman's Rule 2: The War

-Life and Banishment of Apophis: book 1

-The Kidney Friendly Diet

-The Ultimate Hemp Cookbook

-Creating a Dispensary(legally)

-Cleanliness throughout life: the importance of showering from childhood to adulthood.

-Strong Roots: The Risks of Overcoddling children

-Hemp Horoscopes: Cosmic Insights and Earthly Healing

- Celestial Hemp Navigating the Zodiac: Through the Green Cosmos

-Astrological Hemp: Aligning The Stars with Earth's Ancient Herb

-The Astrological Guide to Hemp: Stars, Signs, and Sacred Leaves

-Green Growth: Innovative Marketing Strategies for your Hemp Products and Dispensary

-Cosmic Cannabis

-Astrological Munchies

-Henry The Hemp

-Zodiacal Roots: The Astrological Soul Of Hemp

- **Green Constellations: Intersection of Hemp and Zodiac**

-Hemp in The Houses: An astrological Adventure Through The Cannabis Galaxy

-Galactic Ganja Guide

Heavenly Hemp

Zodiac Leaves

Doctor Who Astrology

Cannastrology

Stellar Satvias and Cosmic Indicas

<u>Celestial Cannabis: A Zodiac Journey</u>

AstroHerbology: The Sky and The Soil: Volume 1

AstroHerbology:Celestial Cannabis:Volume 2

Cosmic Cannabis Cultivation

The Starry Guide to Herbal Harmony: Volume 1

The Starry Guide to Herbal Harmony: Cannabis Universe: Volume 2

Yugioh Astrology: Astrological Guide to Deck, Duels and more

Nightmare Mansion: Echoes of The Abyss

Nightmare Mansion 2: Legacy of Shadows

Nightmare Mansion 3: Shadows of the Forgotten

Nightmare Mansion 4: Echoes of the Damned

The Life and Banishment of Apophis: Book 2

Nightmare Mansion: Halls of Despair

<u>Healing with Herb: Cannabis and Hydrocephalus</u>

<u>Planetary Pot: Aligning with Astrological Herbs: Volume 1</u>

Fast Track to Freedom: 30 Days to Financial Independence Using AI, Assets, and Agile Hustles

<u>Cosmic Hemp Pathways</u>

How to Become Financially Free in 30 Days: 10,000 Paths to Prosperity

Zodiacal Herbage: Astrological Insights: Volume 1

Nightmare Mansion: Whispers in the Walls

The Daleks Invade Atlantis

Henry the hemp and Hydrocephalus

10X The Kidney Friendly Diet

Cannabis Universe: Adult coloring book

Hemp Astrology: The Healing Power of the Stars

Zodiacal Herbage: Astrological Insights: Cannabis Universe: Volume 2

<u>Planetary Pot: Aligning with Astrological Herbs: Cannabis Universes: Volume 2</u>

Doctor Who Meets the Replicators and SG-1: The Ultimate Battle for Survival

Nightmare Mansion: Curse of the Blood Moon

<u>The Celestial Stoner: A Guide to the Zodiac</u>

Cosmic Pleasures: Sex Toy Astrology for Every Sign

Hydrocephalus Astrology: Navigating the Stars and Healing Waters

Lapis and the Mischievous Chocolate Bar

Celestial Positions: Sexual Astrology for Every Sign

Apophis's Shadow Work Journal: : A Journey of Self-Discovery and Healing

Kinky Cosmos: Sexual Kink Astrology for Every Sign

Digital Cosmos: The Astrological Digimon Compendium

Stellar Seeds: The Cosmic Guide to Growing with Astrology

Apophis's Daily Gratitude Journal

Cat Astrology: Feline Mysteries of the Cosmos

The Cosmic Kama Sutra: An Astrological Guide to Sexual Positions

Unleash Your Potential: A Guided Journal Powered by AI Insights

Whispers of the Enchanted Grove

Cosmic Pleasures: An Astrological Guide to Sexual Kinks

369, 12 Manifestation Journal

Whisper of the nocturne journal(blank journal for writing or drawing)

The Boogey Book

Locked In Reflection: A Chastity Journey Through Locktober

Generating Wealth Quickly:

How to Generate $100,000 in 24 Hours

Star Magic: Harness the Power of the Universe

The Flatulence Chronicles: A Fart Journal for Self-Discovery

The Doctor and The Death Moth

Seize the Day: A Personal Seizure Tracking Journal

The Ultimate Boogeyman Safari: A Journey into the Boogie World and Beyond

Whispers of Samhain: 1,000 Spells of Love, Luck, and Lunar Magic: Samhain Spell Book

Apophis's guides:

Witch's Spellbook Crafting Guide for Halloween

<u>Frost & Flame: The Enchanted Yule Grimoire of 1000 Winter Spells</u>

<u>The Ultimate Boogey Goo Guide & Spooky Activities for Halloween Fun</u>

Harmony of the Scales: A Libra's Spellcraft for Balance and Beauty

The Enchanted Advent: 36 Days of Christmas Wonders

Nightmare Mansion: The Labyrinth of Screams

Harvest of Enchantment: 1,000 Spells of Gratitude, Love, and Fortune for Thanksgiving

The Boogey Chronicles: A Journal of Nightly Encounters and Shadowy Secrets

The 12 Days of Financial Freedom: A Step-by-Step Christmas Countdown to Transform Your Finances

Sigil of the Eternal Spiral Blank Journal

A Christmas Feast: Timeless Recipes for Every Meal

Holiday Stress-Free Solutions: A Survival Guide to Thriving During the Festive Season

Yu-Gi-Oh! Holiday Gifting Mastery: The Ultimate Guide for Fans and Newcomers Alike

Holiday Harmony: A Hydrocephalus Survival Guide for the Festive Season

Celestial Craft: The Witch's Almanac for 2025 – A Cosmic Guide to Manifestations, Moons, and Mystical Events

Doctor Who: The Toymaker's Winter Wonderland

Tulsa King Unveiled: A Thrilling Guide to Stallone's Mafia Masterpiece

Pendulum Craft: A Complete Guide to Crafting and Using Personalized Divination Tools

Nightmare Mansion: Santa's Eternal Eve

Starlight Noel: A Cosmic Journey through Christmas Mysteries

The Dark Architect: Unlocking the Blueprint of Existence

Surviving the Embrace: The Ultimate Guide to Encounters with The Hugging Molly

The Enchanted Codex: Secrets of the Craft for Witches, Wiccans, and Pagans

Harvest of Gratitude: A Complete Thanksgiving Guide

Yuletide Essentials: A Complete Guide to an Authentic and Magical Christmas

Celestial Smokes: A Cosmic Guide to Cigars and Astrology

Living in Balance: A Comprehensive Survival Guide to Thriving with Diabetes Insipidus

Cosmic Symbiosis: The Venom Zodiac Chronicles

The Cursed Paw of Ambition

Cosmic Symbiosis: The Astrological Venom Journal

Celestial Wonders Unfold: A Stargazer's Guide to the Cosmos (2024-2029)

The Ultimate Black Friday Prepper's Guide: Mastering Shopping Strategies and Savings

Cosmic Sales: The Astrological Guide to Black Friday Shopping
Legends of the Corn Mother and Other Harvest Myths
Whispers of the Harvest: The Corn Mother's Journal
The Evergreen Spellbook
The Doctor Meets the Boogeyman
The White Witch of Rose Hall's SpellBook
The Gingerbread Golem's Shadow: A Study in Sweet Darkness
The Gingerbread Golem Codex: An Academic Exploration of Sweet Myths
The Gingerbread Golem Grimoire: Sweet Magicks and Spells for the Festive Witch
The Curse of the Gingerbread Golem
10-minute Christmas Crafts for kids
<u>Christmas Crisis Solutions: The Ultimate Last-Minute Survival Guide</u>
Gingerbread Golem Recipes: Holiday Treats with a Magical Twist
The Infinite Key: Unlocking Mystical Secrets of the Ages
Enchanted Yule: A Wiccan and Pagan Guide to a Magical and Memorable Season
Dinosaurs of Power: Unlocking Ancient Magick
Astro-Dinos: The Cosmic Guide to Prehistoric Wisdom
Gallifrey's Yule Logs: A Festive Doctor Who Cookbook
The Dino Grimoire: Secrets of Prehistoric Magick
The Gift They Never Knew They Needed
The Gingerbread Golem's Culinary Alchemy: Enchanting Recipes for a Sweetly Dark Feast
A Time Lord Christmas: Holiday Adventures with the Doctor
Krampusproofing Your Home: Defensive Strategies for Yule
Silent Frights: A Collection of Christmas Creepypastas to Chill Your Bones
Santa Raptor's Jolly Carnage: A Dino-Claus Christmas Tale
Prehistoric Palettes: A Dino Wicca Coloring Journey
The Christmas Wishkeeper Chronicles

The Starlight Sleigh: A Holiday Journey
Elf Secrets: The True Magic of the North Pole
Candy Cane Conjurations
Cooking with Kids: Recipes Under 20 Minutes
Doctor Who: The TARDIS Confiscation
The Anxiety First Aid Kit: Quick Tools to Calm Your Mind
Frosty Whispers: A Winter's Tale
The Infinite Key: Unlocking the Secrets to Prosperity, Resilience, and Purpose
The Grasping Void: Why You'll Regret This Purchase
Astrology for Busy Bees: Star Signs Simplified
The Instant Focus Formula: Cut Through the Noise
The Secret Language of Colors: Unlocking the Emotional Codes
Sacred Fossil Chronicles: Blank Journal
The Christmas Cottage Miracle
Feeding Frenzy: Graboid-Inspired Recipes
Manifest in Minutes: The Quick Law of Attraction Guide
The Symbiote Chronicles: Doctor Who's Venomous Journey
Think Tiny, Grow Big: The Minimalist Mindset
The Energy Key: Unlocking Limitless Motivation
New Year, New Magic: Manifesting Your Best Year Yet

If you want solar for your home go here: https://www.harborso-lar.live/apophisenterprises/

Get Some Tarot cards: https://www.makeplayingcards.com/sell/apophis-occult-shop

Get some shirts: https://www.bonfire.com/store/apophis-shirt-emporium/

<u>Instagrams:</u>
@apophis_enterprises,
@apophisbookemporium,
@apophisscardshop
Twitter: @apophisenterpr1
 Tiktok:@apophisenterprise
Youtube: @sg1fan23477, @FiresideRetreatKingdom
Hive: @sg1fan23477
CheeLee: @SG1fan23477

Podcast: Apophis Chat Zone: https://open.spotify.com/show/
5zXbrCLEV2xzCp8ybrfHsk?si=fb4d4fdbdce44dec

Newsletter: https://apophiss-newsletter-27c897.beehiiv.com/

If you want to support me or see posts of other projects that I have come over to: **buymeacoffee.com/mpetchinskg**
I post there daily several times a day

Get your Dinowicca or Christmas themed digital products, especially Santa Raptor songs and other musics. Here: **https://sg1fan23477.gumroad.com**

Apophis Yuletide Digital has not only digital Christmas items, but it will have all things with Dinowicca as well as other Digital products.